AYUH, ANOTHER DOWNEAST COOKBOOK

VIRGINIA BROWN WRIGHT

AYUH, ANOTHER DOWNEAST COOKBOOK
RECIPES FROM MAINE

CreateSpace Independent Publishing Platform
North Charleston, South Carolina

Ayuh, Another Downeast Cookbook

Recipes From Maine

by Virginia Brown Wright

Cover designed by:Virginia Brown Wright

Cover text edited by: Ingrid Hall

www.luv2write.net

Dedication

David, Robbie, and Shane
With All My Love

CreateSpace Independent Publishing Platform
North Charleston, SC

First Paperback Edition 2018

ISBN-I3:978-I490950815
ISBN-I0: 978-I490950818
LCCN:201492I079

More books by this author available online:
http://www.amazon.com/author/virginiawright
http://www.barnesandnoble.com
http://www.booksamillion.com

My Families Table

Many years ago, wild game provided meat for my families table. Living in Maine, my father was a hunter. He got his fair share of deer each season. Hunting for game birds like partridge and small animals such as rabbit was another way to provide. He loved going fishing for bass and brook trout, too. And when he hit the tides just right, he would load the car up with his hip boots, grab the clam hoe and roller, and hit the clam flats for a mess of clams. This isn't just how our family got their food and ate, for many generations, people from Maine have hunted and fished here. Lakes in Maine flourish with abundant fish, wild game from deer to bear, and moose are found in the wilderness here. Trapping beaver and muskrat is something some of the most rugged Mainers attempt, including my father-in-law. Today, hunting, fishing, lobstering, and clamming, still plays a significant role in the state—it is the Maine way.

Ayuh, Another Downeast Cookbook: Recipes From Maine will bring you delicious and unique recipes with every page you turn, including-- Venison Jerky, Coon Cacciatore, Swiss Moose Steak, Smothered Muskrat, Chestnut Stuffing n' Partridge, Lobster casserole, and more.

-Virginia Wright

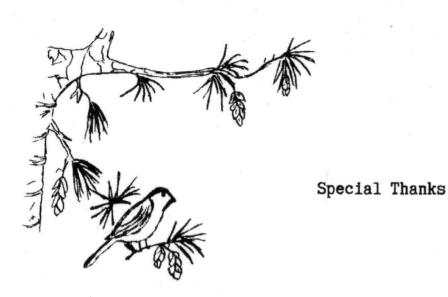

Special Thanks

My thanks go out to all who contributed recipes, ideas, suggestions, and spent time making Ayuh, Another Downeast Cookbook: Recipes from Maine possible. To Bud Leavitt - BDN's outdoor columnist and TV host, members of The Maine Professional Guides Association, members of Maine Lobstermen's Association, Linwood Rideout and the B & A Railroad, Bob Wright-Arborist and Forester. Also, to Charles Zurhorst, former Maine Guide, Author, and teacher, for all his advice, guidance and reassurance.

A shout out with gratitude to all the people in Washington and Waldo Counties that sent in recipes.

Many thanks go out to Diana Ryan for depicting Maine with her many illustrations scattered throughout Ayuh, Another Downeast Cookbook Recipes From Maine. These will be noted as D. Ryan.

Lastly, thanks to my husband, David, and sons Robbie and Shane for bearing with me during the making of this book.

Cooking Tips & Tricks

Baked Duck

The key to a well baked and tasty Duck, is to make double sure
the bird is clean. inside and out, no pin feathers, and no blood,
just thoroughly washed and cared for. Stuff and bake exactly the
way you would a chicken, and add a couple of strips of bacon on
top.

> Linwood Rideout, Former Maine Guide
> Bowdoinham, Maine
> Guiding Since 1938

Cooking on a Flat Rock

Steaks, chops, ham, venison, hamburger, frankfurters and such
things as swordfish, haddock, tuna steaks, etc. may also be
cooked satisfactorily on a flat rock. Be sure to pick out hard
packed rock that will not burst easily under heat. Eschew shale
slate, flaky stone and porous rock.

Heat the flat rock thoroughly so that it will sizzle when you
sprinkle a few drops of water on it, then rub a slice of pineapple
and a bit of garlic or onion over the steak, ham or fish; grease
your rock grid with bacon rind or butter, then proceed to cook.
The trick lies in keeping an even heat of hot coals and avoiding
a blistering blaze whose heat will shatter your improvised utensil
not only to send your steak flying, but to invite injury from
bursting particles of rock. Is good! Try it.

Guide's Biscuits

Three cups sifted flour, one teaspoon salt, two level tablespoons
baking powder, three tablespoons lard, one cup milk(wherever
milk is indicated, equal parts of evaporated milk and water is
meant, in the absence of whole milk).Or, one cup cold water in
place of milk. Mix dry ingredients, add unmelted shortening by
working in with fingers, taking care to leave no large lumps;
mix in liquid to make a sodt dough that you can handle, and dump
on floured board. Knead the mass just enough to make a smooth ball,
then roll and cut. Baking tin should be warm, not hot, and well
greased. Bake before a hot fire and, as they begin to brown, smear
lightly with melted butter.We like to think that rubbing in the
unmelted lard makes for flakier and lighter biscuits.In the absence
of baking powder, use one teaspoon baking soda and two teaspoons
cream of tarter.)If you have good luck and have a good baking fire
watch'em closely, for they'll be so light and flaky that a good
puff of wind will send them flying over the tree tops!

Tea-Coffee-Cocoa

Most woodsmen prefer tea to coffee or cocoa, out on the trail.
Tea is a fine stimulant and the midday lunch is not complete
without a steaming hot cup of the brew, if conditions allow.
Tea should be steeped and not boiled. Wintergreen leaves and
berries make a good substitute, in a pinch.

Recipes and Tips contributed by:Linwood Rideout, Former Maine Guide,
taken from book "In The Maine Woods",edited by B. & A. Railroad in
1942.

Maple Syrup

Pure sap syrup, of course, holds first place; but a fair substi
tute can be made from imitation maple flavor and either white or
brown sugar. We recommend that you allow the syrup to cool, after
boiling, before adding the flavor. Lacking flavor, a fine syrup
can be made in the woods by using cane sugar and caramel, which
is nothing but burnt sugar, for coloring.
Here's a woodsman's kink--cut a six or eight inch sugar maple and
bark it, then knock off a pile of chips, and place them in a ket
tle and let them boil for about fifteen minutes at which time
skim and replace with freshly cut chips, heap them up and, as the
water boils away, it will retain the maple flavor. The operation
will take time and patience, but so does the boiling down of sap
in the manufacture of syrup!When you have thus extracted enough
flavor, add enough sugar syrup to thicken and you will have a
passable mixture that will fool even an expert.

Cereals--Prunes

Because of their bulk, dry cereals are seldom taken along. Most
woods cooks prefer to make their own from rolled oats, cream of
Wheat, Wheatens, etc. City folks, however, find it hard to get
used to cereals without cream or whole milk usually. Boiled rice,
 rice and tapioca, and corn meal mush make a fine morning dish,
while the left-overs can be fried in butter.
Prunes are staple. Wash and soak well and while stewing, add a
slice of lemon and a couple of cloves. Don't add sugaar until
they are cool. (Try dumping a handful of well-washed raisins in
the rolled oats.)

Barbecue Pit

One of the best places to build a barbecue pit is against a stone
wall, some four feet high. Rock at the sides to make a three-sided
reflector, and arrange the turning spit just in front. Drilled
holes in the pipe (spit) will allow the use of iron skewers to
hold the meat, which should be held firmly in order to turn,strong
wire will answer.

Recipes and tips contributed by: Linwood Rideout, Former Maine Guide
Taken from book "In The Maine Woods", edited by B. & A. Railroad in
1942.

Camper's Specials

Camp Coffee

To fix coffee over a campfire, use a percolator style coffee pot. Fill the pot with water to just below the spout. Fill the basket with coffee grounds and insert into the water. Use two tablespoons of coffee grounds per serving. Perk coffee over your heat source for about eight to ten minutes. Before serving, let the coffee settle before pouring, so that grounds don't end up in your coffee cup.

Campfire Foil Potatoes

Baking potato
Bacon grease, leftover from morning breakfast
Salt and Pepper

Instructions:

Clean and dry potatoes, then rub the bacon grease all over the potato. Season the outside of the potato with salt and pepper. Tear off a sheet of aluminum foil and tightly wrap the potato like a blanket folding the ends up. Place the wrapped potato in the coals of a campfire. Cook until fork tender.

—Number of servings depends on how many people sitting around the campfire. Rule of thumb is one potato per person.

Fried Potatoes with Bacon

Bacon, crumbled and reserve the grease
Potatoes, one for each person
Salt and pepper, to taste

In an iron skillet, cook bacon, take out the bacon and set aside. Peel and cut potatoes into thin slices, add to the bacon fat. Cook potatoes turning often. Done when fork tender. Two to three minutes before taking the fried potatoes out, add crumbled bacon, toss lightly. Salt and pepper, to taste. The number of potatoes used is based on how many people you are serving. You can adjust potatoes and bacon according to numbers.

BANGOR DAILY NEWS MONDAY OCTOBER 3, 1983   17

Maine Guide Suzanne Hockmeyer of The Forks uses' the following recipe, which is taken from "Ayuh, Another Downeast Cookbook," by Virginia Brown Wright of Orono.

SUZIE'S KENNEBEC GORP

4 cups coconut
4 cups raisins
2 pounds granola
4 cups M&M's
2 pounds peanuts

Combine ingredients. Make eight quarts. Package into 1-quart plastic bags. One package serves 8-10 people.

When submitting this recipe, Suzie noted that once the mix is packaged up this snack serves "one soft load!"

Thanks, Suzie. I tried this mix and love it. I agree when carrying it in your backpack it is a lightweight snack. :-) -Virginia

What is Gorp?

Gorp is another name for trail mix. Mixing nuts, seeds, and dried fruit makes for an excellent high-energy snack on the trail.

Bear - Moose - Muskrat
Rabbit - Raccoon
Venison

Roast Bear

5 to 6 pound bear roast
2 pounds onions, sliced
large can tomatoes
salt and pepper to taste

Mash tomatoes, or cut up and pour over roast with sliced onions. Baste occasionally. Cook at 250 degrees for 8 hours.

Charles L. Davis,Maine Guide, Waterville,Maine

© Virginia Wright

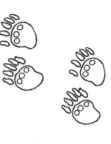

Venison Hamburg and Macaroni Special:

1 pound deer hamburg
1 can sloppy joe sauce
2 cups macaroni (cooked)
1 pint of Garden Special
1 tablespoon vegetable oil

Brown deerburger in vegetable oil, add sloppy joe sauce and garden special to hamburg. Simmer for 5 minutes and serve hot.

Garden special:

2 pecks ripe tomatoes
3 pounds onions
8 green peppers
1 package celery
8 red peppers
1 teaspoon salt
1 teaspoon sugar to each quart that you do.

Prepare vegetables to grind with coarse blade in grinder. Simmer on stove in a canner for ½ hour. Stir occasionally. Put in hot processed jars and seal tightly.

Madeline Patten, Belfast, Maine

Venison Jerky

2 pounds venison
1 teaspoon seasoned salt
1 teaspoon onion powder
½ teaspoon garlic powder
¼ teaspoon pepper
½ cup Worcestershire sauce
½ cup soy sauce

Cut venison into quarter-inch slices along grain (it is easier to slice if partially frozen). Combine dry and liquid ingredients to make a marinade. Marinate meat overnight in the refrigerator. Drain. Lay meat strips on an oven rack and place foil on the bottom rack to catch drippings. Leave the door ajar. Set oven at 150 degrees. Dry meat for 6 hours. Turn oven and leave meat in oven for another 6 hours.

Bob Paradis,Rangely Region Outfitters,Maine Guide,Oquossoc,Maine

Venison Meatloaf

2 pounds deerburger
1 cup cracker crumbs
¼ teaspoon pepper
1 teaspoon hamburg seasoniong
1/8 cup olive oil
3 eggs,slightly beaten
1 medium onion,chopped fine
1 teaspoon salt
1/8 cup milk

Mix all ingredients well. Form into loaf pan and bake in 375 degree oven approximately 45 to 60 minutes.

Clarence Brown Sr.,Belfast,Maine

Venison Mincemeat

2 pounds meat (cooked)

1 pound suet, salt pork, or butter

1 pint vinegar

1 pint molasses

1 tablespoon ground cloves

1 tablespoon allspice

2 ounces lemon juice

5 pounds apples

2 pounds raisins,seedless

1 quart of cider,or juice from apples

1 tablespoon salt

1 tablespoon nutmeg

2 tablespoons cinnamon

Put meat, apples and suet(if you use) through meat grinder.
Combine all ingredients in large kettle and simmer until done,
(4-5 hours). Extra vinegar may be added for tartness. Leftover
parts of jars of jelly or jam or any fruit you might have, If
you use oranges, grind up peels also. Instead of extra vinegar,
may add extra apples. If you can't get raisins substitute currants.
Store in refrigerator in a large glass covered container. Pickle
jars are good. Will fill several 9' pies.

Sheila B. Howie, Belfast, Maine

Roast Venison

1 venison roast, trimmed. Use mixture of dash of salt, pepper, 1/4 cup grated onion, and flour according to size of roast. Cover with thin layers of salt pork. Put 1/2 cup of water in roaster, cook in oven of not more than 350 degrees. Do not cover roast. After roast is brown, baste with venison sauce. Should require 25 minutes per pound. May add water to make gravy.

Venison Sauce

1/2 cup onion (grated)
1/2 stick celery (chopped)
2 tablespoons butter
1/2 teaspoon salt
1 cup boiling water
dash pepper

Mix all ingredients, and simmer until done. This sauce may be used for any wild game.

Sheila B. Howie, Belfast, Maine

Venison Soup

1 pound trimmed venison,cubed
4 beef bouillon cubes
3/4 cup fresh or frozen peas
1 small onion,diced
1 tablespoon parsley
4 cups water
3 medium potatos,diced
3-4 fresh carrots,sliced
4 tablespoons butter
salt and pepper to taste

Saute' onion in melted butter in pot; then add deer meat and brown. Add rest of ingredients and simmer 1 hour on medium heat in covered pot. Shake parmesian cheese over soup, and serve with hot biscuits.

Robert W. Wright, Forester and Arborist, East Machias, Maine

Smothered Venison

2 pounds of boneless lean venison
3 cans of small silver onions
½ cup olive oil
1 teaspoon whole pickling spice
1 medium can of tomatoes
½ cup of vinegar
5 cloves of garlic
salt and pepper to taste

Cut meat in small pieces. Brown slightly in oil. Add onion juice of one can to meat, together with spice (tied in small clean cheese cloth) vinegar, tomatoes, garlic and seasoning. Cover tightly and cook until meat is half done. Add onions and cook until meat and onions are tender and liquid is reduced to a delicious gravy. Remove spices at once.

Roxanne B. Carter, Swanville, Maine

Wrapped Rabbit

1 rabbit boned and tenderized with fork. Sufficent bacon slices to wrap pieces of rabbit. Place on aluminum foil in oven of 350 degrees, or in aluminum foil wrapped loosely and placed on camp grill. Slowly cook until done.

Barbecued Rabbit

1/3 cup Teriyaki sauce
1 clove garlic - chopped
1 dash pepper
1 rabbit quartered or boned

1/3 cup barbecue sauce
1 dash salt
2 ziploc bags (bigger than sandwich)
1 piece of aluminum foil large enough
to cover rabbit pieces on grill

1 plastic bag filled with charcoal

Mix marinade of above ingredients and place in ziploc bag. Marinade can be thinned slightly with water but should not lose body. Tenderize rabbit pieces with fork and place in ziploc bag containing marinade. This bag can be put into the second ziploc to prevent leakage or spillage while in your back pack. Marinade overnight or from morning to evening. At the end of the day or while ice fishing or whatever. Start charcoals and set backpack grill. Place pieces of rabbit on grill and cook slow. Save marinade and use to baste, take aluminum foil and tear slightly in center for vent, place over rabbit and grill to hold heat and smoke.
DEPENDING ON WHO AND WHERE A RED WINE (MARGAUX '67) COMPLIMENTS THESE RECIPES!

Steve Pacuska,Maine Guide,Lincoln, Maine

Jugged Rabbit

Cut two or three rabbits into serving pieces and brown in butter.
Place the pieces in a covered casserole dish and cover with chicken broth that has been combined with 1 cup of dry red wine. Add
a large, quartered onion and salt and pepper to taste. Cook for
three hours in a 275 degree oven. When done, pour the gravy into
a pan and simmer. Make a paste with 3 tablespoons of butter and
3 tablespoons flour and stir into the gravy to thicken. Pour gravy
over the rabbit and serve.

Bob Paradis, Maine Guide, Oquossoc, Maine

Smothered Rabbit or Squirrel

Dress and clean rabbit or squirrel, wipe clean with damp cloth
and cut in pieces for serving. Disjoint legs at body and second
joints; split down center back thru breast and cut each half in
two pieces. Dip pieces into seasoned flour; brown in hot fat.
Reduce heat and cook until tender, about 1 hour. If rabbit or
squirrel is old or of uncertain age, add small amount of hot
water; cover tightly in pot, and cook over low heat 1½ hours.

Robert W. Wright, Forester and Arborist, East Machias, Maine

Bud Leavitt's Barbecued Steak

2 pounds moose, deer steak

¼ cup catsup

¼ salad oil

3 tablespoons lemon juice

2 tablespoons vinegar

2 tablespoons hickory liquid

3 drops tabasco sauce

1 teaspoon worcestershire sauce

1 teaspoon salt

¼ teaspoon onion powder

½ teaspoon powdered mustard

¼ teaspoon paprika

1 clove garlic, chopped fine

Combine ingredients and pour over steaks in a shallow baking pan.
Let stand 30 minutes, turning once. Place steaks in well-greased
hinged wire grills. Cook about 4 inches from hot coals about 8
minutes, basting as steaks cook. Turn and cook other side an
equal time.

(you can use the same ingredients and cooking methods on fish
steaks, i,e., Atlantic salmon, lake trout, striped bass, pike,
muskellunge and other fishes, I suspect. I have used salmon
and lake trout and the results are an amazingly tangy fish steak.)

Bud Leavitt, Outdoor Editor, Bangor Daily News, Bangor, Maine

Swiss Moose Steak

Several large slices 3/8" to ½ inch thick moose steak (2-3) pounds
1 tablespoon brown sugar
1 large can stewed tomatoes
1 bay leaf
4 teaspoon corn meal
1 clove garlic diced
1 large onion sliced
4 stalks celery diced
3 shakes worcestershire sauce
2 dash soy sauce
pinch of thyme
salt and pepper to taste
1 pinch onion salt
1 can beef consomme' or beef drippings (cup)

Cut meat into individual portions and pound with meat hammer
or edge of saucer until meat fiber is broken. Brown meat with
garlic and onions in butter or oil after sprinkling onion with
sugar. Add consomme', Beef drippings, bay leaf, thyme, soy sauce,
celery, and cornmeal. Then cook 2 hrs. covered. Add tomatoes,
cook uncovered for 1 hour at 350 degrees, or until tender. Make
sure liquid does not evaporate, add small amount of water or
tomato juice if necessary. Serve with boiled potatoes, carrots,
etc., This can also, be used for deer meat or beef and you can
use cuts that are a little tougher than for steak.

Charles (Bud) Dillihunt, Maine Guide, Jackman, Maine

Muskrat

Served in Fall during trapping season. In the south Muskrat is
called swamp rabbit. Cut muskrat into 4 sections; 2 hind legs
and divide saddle cross wise. Trim off flap and ribs. I don't
use front legs. Soak in salted water over night. Dry meat sections. Brown or sear in frying pan in hot bacon fat or corn oil.
Then cover with water to which is added, a teaspoon of thyme,
pepper to taste and $\frac{1}{4}$ cup soy sauce. Let simmer on back of stove,
for 2 to 3 hours or until meat falls away from bone. Serve meat
and gravy on hot soda biscuits. Allow one muskrat per hungry
hunter or trapper for night meal.

Norm Bradley, Maine Guide, Norridgewock, Maine

Coon Cacciatore

1 medium size raccoon
1 teaspoon salt
½ teaspoon pepper
½ teaspoon thyme
1 teaspoon oregano
½ teaspoon garlic salt
1 teaspoon mint leaves
2 beef bouillon cubes
1 package lipton onion soup
2 large cans tomato juice
10 large carrots
1 medium turnip
3 medium onions
10 medium potatoes
8 parsnips
2 green peppers
2 quarts water

Skin and remove all fat from raccoon. Boil with 1 teaspoon salt
until all meat comes off the bone. Chop raccoon in small pieces.
Put in canner with diced vegetables,spices,lipton onion soup,
bouillon cubes, and add remaining ingredients. Bring all ingredients to a boil, then reduce heat and simmer 1½ hours. Good with
dumplings.
Makes approx. 4 gallons.

Madeline Patten, Belfast, Maine

Chestnut Stuffing n' Partridge

Chestnuts, 1 quart
1/3 cup bread crumbs
2 tablespoons butter
¼ teaspoon butter
1 teaspoon onion, minced
1 teaspoon celery, minced
1 teaspoon salt
2 tablespoons cream

Shell and blanch the chestnuts, then cook in boiling water until tender. Mash and rub thru colander and mix well with the other ingredients. Use as stuffing for partride. Thyme may be used as seasoning instead of onion.

Sheila B. Howie, Belfast, Maine

Broiled Partridge

Broiled partridge or quail stew are prepared like squab-size chickens, split down the back, brushed with butter, seasoned and broiled, then served on toast, a whole bird to each hungry hunter or trapper. A tart jelly such as red plum, or green gage plum, or cranberry jelly, should be served with wild rice and sauted in butter.

E. Virginia Glass, Belfast, Maine

Italian Partridge Breast

2 partridge Breast cooked and diced
1 medium onion
Dash oregano, sweet basil, paprika, and last but, not least 10 tbsp.
Italian dressing (Phaiffers)
Do not add salt til ready for table. Simmer for about 10 minutes.
Serve with mashed Maine potatoes or rice pilaf.

Katherine A. Hegarty, Registered Maine Guide, Jackman, Maine

Partridge Stew

2 partridge
1 large onion
3 potatoes, cut into small pieces
4 stalks celery, chopped into large pieces
1 parsnip, cut into small rounds
4 carrots, cut into small rounds
1 jar canned green beans (optional)
salt and pepper
celery salt
4 chicken bouillion cubes

Cook cleaned partridge in large kettle of salt and water about 1 hour or until meat falls off bone. Remove from water. Skim water and remove particles. Bone partridge. Add all ingredients to stock plus partridge meat. Simmer about 2 hours at low heat or 1 hour at high heat. Serve with hot biscuits and saucers of molasses to dip biscuits in. Serves 4 hungry hunters or trappers. Partridge can be replaced with rabbit.

Norm Bradley, Maine Guide, Norridgewock, Maine

Partridge Salad

Grouse meat (leftover) diced
Onion, 1 hard boiled egg, celery, cukes, radished-all diced,also.

Mix together all above ingredients, add any of your favorite
dressing. I love it wirh mayonnaise. In the woods we use no
dressing. Lettuce or potatoes, diced, (optional).

Katherine A. Hegarty, Registered Maine Guide, Jackman, Maine

Partridge Tidbits

Quarter partridge breasts. Wrap with bacon and fasten with tooth
picks. Bake in 400 degree oven for 20 minutes.

Bob Paradis, Rangely Region Outfitters, Maine Guide, Oquossoc, Maine

Baked Pheasant

Clean, remove pinions, and split the bird down the back. Rub
with salt and pepper, brush over with melted butter, dredge
with flour and surround with trimmings of fat salt pork. Bake
40 minutes in a moderate oven (375 degrees) , basting 3 or 4
times. Arrange the bird on a platter and garnish with parsley.

Pheasant With Hunters Dressing

½ pound pork sausage
1 cup chunkys style applesauce
¼ cup chopped parsley
¼ cup sherry
2 cups bread,cubed
1/3 cup chopped onion
¼ teaspoon sage
¼ teaspoon salt
3 pound pheasant

Dress and clean pheasant. Fill cavity loosely with dressing.Pour
sherry over bird. Bake in 350 degree oven for about 1 hour; or
until done.

Sheila B. Howie, Belfast, Maine

Baked Woodcock

Flour meat well. Braise in heavy skillet. Place in covered dish
and bake slowly in moderate oven of 350 degrees, until tender.
May have to add a little stock or butter. Baking time, approx.
1½ hours.

Bob Paradis, Rangely Region Outfitters, Maine Guide, Oquossoc, Maine

Timberdoodle Stew

Saute' 6 woodcock until tender and meat can be picked off. Save
juice, add 1 cup water, 1 bouillon cube, 2 carrots, 2 sliced
onions,cut up small, ½ cup barley. Cook until done to taste. Add
a little wine if desired, but, also save a little for the cook.

Frank Gilley, Maine Guide, Brewer, Maine

Baked Duck

There is widespread misconception that duck, particularly
diving ducks, such as Mergansers, will taste fishy and gamey
when cooked. Totally untrue.

It's critical to dress the duck out, or preferably just breast
it, withim moments of shooting it. I maintain that ducks, especially Mergansers or other divers, will acquire that fishy, sour
taste only if the duck is left to sit without cleaning. And it
doesn't take long for the meat to become tainted.

As for cooking, first parboil the breast or clean duck in salted
water. Place it in tinfoil and cover it with molasses. Lay a few
pineapple rings on top, some of thepineapple juice around. Season
to taste with salt, pepper, paprika, even a bit of curry. If you
like it especially sweet, then add some brown sugar, too. Wrap it
up and let bake slowly in the coals. (a single duck should take
about 25 minutes.)

Martin Brown, Maine Guide, Cathance Lake, Grove, Maine

Wild Duck With Sauerkraut

Cook 1 quart of kraut with 1 apple and 1 onion chopped fine, and
a small piece of spareribs for 1 hour. Remove the ribs, strain
the liquid from the kraut to use for basting, and stuff the ducks
with the kraut. This amount will stuff the 3 average-size ducks
with the kraut. Place a strip of bacon or salt pork across the
breast of each and roast in a hot oven (400 degrees to sear, then
reduce heat to 325 degrees.) Reduce the oven heat after ½ hour
and bake slowly until tender. Young ducks will roast in 1½ hours,
old ones require from 30 to 45 minutes longer. Baste frequently
and remove from the oven as soon as tender, as too long a baking
makes the meat dry.

E. Virginia Glass, Belfast, Maine

Maine Wild Greens

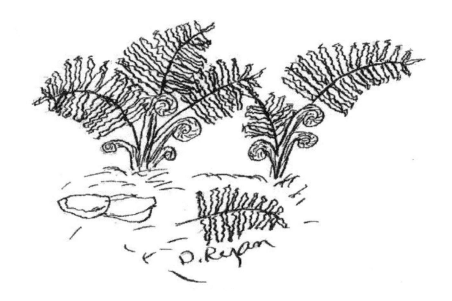

Fiddleheads

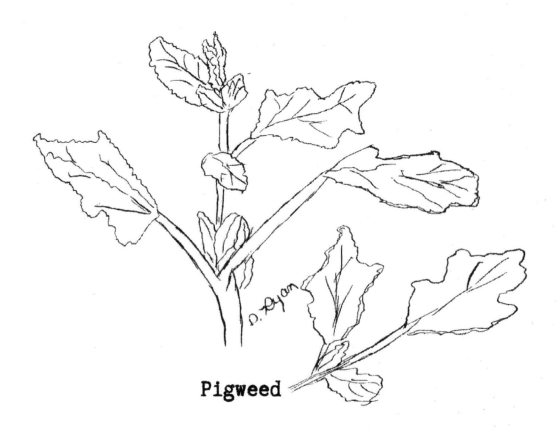

Pigweed

Goose Grass Greens

Goose Grass greens are found on salt water marsh meadows. Best
picked by the fourth of July. Pick or cut greens, discard root
and buds. Wash thouroughly. Bring to a boil in covered pot, in
small amount of water. Simmer for 30 to 40 minutes or until tender. Salt pork or 3-4 slices of bacon may be added for taste.

Robert W. Wright, Forester and Arborist, East Machias, Maine

Fiddleheads-A different vegetable

Fiddleheads are found at the base of the ostrich fern, which grows
in many areas of Maine. Fiddleheads are easily recognized because
they look like the tuning end of a fiddle. They should be picked
before they grow any higher than six inches, and while they are
still curled up and rusty looking. After picking them, rub them
lightly between your hands to remove the"rusty" covering; then
cut away the leafy portion and clean the fuzz from the stem. After
this, simply drop them in boiling salted water and let them simmer
for just about 10 minutes. Remove and serve with bacon drippings
or butter (if you have it) poured over them.

You'll find them different and delicious.

Charles Zurhorst, Former Maine Guide-Jackman area, Roque Bluffs, Maine

Pigweed

Pigweed grows from spring to fall. Pick tops and single leaves,it
shrinks s the pick plenty. The leaves are dull green with white dusting,
unerneath the leaves are unedible. Wash and cook 10 minutes. Serve
with butter,vinegar or as you would spinach. Freezes well. Blanche
to shrink; drain and freeze in ziploc freezer bags.

Robert W. Wright, Forester and Arborist, East Machias, Maine

Crab filling   Good with toasted Eng. Muffins

1 cup crab meat
2 eggs
2 cans chicken soup
1 cup cheese, cut up, fine
1 pint milk
½ lb. butter

Melt cheese, add soup and milk, with eggs beaten in it. Thicken with flour; add crab meat and serve.

Ervena Ames, Thomaston, Maine

Camper's Guide

Baking Times For Cooking Over Coals; Wrap fish in foil.

Fish - Whole - 20 to 30 Minutes according to size. Do not overcook.
Fish - Steaks - 10 to 15 Minutes
Fish - Fillets - 10 to 12 Minutes

Shore Lunch

Ingredients: matches, kool handle fry pan, 3# crisco can(kettle),
½ lb. bacon, water, hand full of loose tea, and at least one com-
petent fisherman.

Directions: Build small protected fire, usually with wet wood and
matches. Set kettle full of water over fire, usually to one side
so when it boils over you don't put the fire out. Clean 4; 10 - 12
inch trout. If last ingredient is missing, open hidden can of spam.
Cook bacon, save grease, throw handfull of tea into kettle, cook
trout in grease. Lay back, pick the bones clean, let tea grounds
settle, finish with tea and short nap (optional depending on fishing.)

Matt Libby, Maine Guide, Masardis, Maine

Bud Leavitt's French Fry in Egg Batter

2 pounds of perch fillets
beef oil
2 eggs
Onion powder to taste
½ cup white flour
½ cup fine bread crumbs
juice of one lemon

Heat 2 or 3 inches of oil until it is almost, but not smoking
(about 375 degrees) Combine eggs, lemon juice and onion powder.
Combine flour and bread crumbs. Place fillets in wire frying
basket and lower gently into oil. Make sure fish is totally imm-
ersed. Fry about 4 minutes or until it acquires color and tex-
ture you like. Drain on absorbent paper and serve.

Bud Leavitt, Outdoor Editor, Bangor Daily News, Bangor, Maine

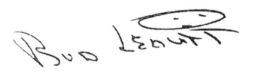

Crab Quiche I

Pastry for 9 inch one crust pie
1 can (7½ oz.) crabmeat (drained)
4 eggs
1½ teaspoons salt
1 can shredded swiss cheese - 4 oz.
½ cup chopped onions
1½ cups milk
¼ teaspoon pepper

Prepare pastry, pat crabmeat dry with papertowels. Crumble and place crabmeat, cheese, and onion on pastry. Beat eggs slightly, beat in remaining ingredients, pour egg mixture into pie plate. Cook uncovered in 425 degree oven for 15 minutes. Reduce oven temp. to 300 degree oven, cook uncovered until knife inserted halfway between center and edge comes out clean. About 30 min., or more. Let stand 10 minutes before cutting.

Crab Quiche II

1 9" or 10" pie shell. Line with foil and weight with rice, beans or pie weights. Bake in 425 degree oven for 8 minutes. Remove foil and weights; cool. In blender, mix ingredients below until smooth.

½ cup mayonaise (preferably Cain's)
2 eggs
½ cup milk
1 tablespoon cornstarch
Add to blender ingredients below, and blend at low speed 2 or 3 seconds, just to mix;

1 cup crabmeat
1/3 cup chopped onion
1½ cups grated cheddar cheese
Dash fresh ground pepper

Pour blender mixture into pie shell. Bake in 350 degree oven for 35 to 40 minutes until top is puffed up and golden brown. Remove to pantry and allow 10 minutes resting time, so, custard will set. If by some unlikely chance there's any leftover, freeze in indiv-

Crabmeat Quiche II continued

idual slices, warming later in microwave for a lunch.) Serve with garden cukes or tossed salad. Especially tasty if you pick your own crabs.

Ossie and Nancy Beal, Beals, Maine

Deviled Crab

1 cup cream
3 tablespoons butter
2 tablespoons flour
1¼ cups crabmeat
1 tablespoons chopped parsley
4 hard boiled egg yolks, shreded fine

Mix all ingredients, Season to taste. Place in buttered baking dish, dot with butter and sprinkle with bread crumbs. Bake in moderate oven (375 degrees) for 30 minutes.

E. Virginia Glass, Belfast, Maine,

Crabmeat and Macaroni Salad

½ package cooked macaroni
½ green pepper, minced
¼ cup onion, minced
½ pound crabmeat
mayonaise to taste (approximate ½ cup)

Mix all ingredients, serve cold on lettuce, or as is.

Sheila Howie, Belfast, Maine

Clam Fritters

1 pound clams, ground up
1 cup milk
1 medium onion, ground up
2 eggs
2 cups sifted flour
1 teaspoon baking powder
½ teaspoon salt
2 tablespoons dry milk
pepper to taste

Mix liquid and dry ingredients separately. Gradually add dry to liquid, stirring constantly. Heat griddle or cast iron fry pan with cooking oil. Fry fritters, dropping batter by spoonfuls, until inside is no longer soggy. Serve with catsup and cold slaw. Feeds family of four and one golden retriever.

Ossie and Nancy Beal, Beals, Maine

Escalloped Clams

1 quart clams
3 cups cracker crumbs
½ cup butter, melted
1 pint warm milk
2 eggs, beaten
¼ cup clam liquor

Mix all ingredients together, clams and liquid last. Bake in casserole dish in 350 degree oven for 45 minutes.

E. Virginia Glass, Belfast, Maine

Codfish Baked With Lemon

1 pound cod fillets
2 tablespoons lemon juice
¼ cup melted butter
¼ cup flour
salt,pepper,paprika (sprinkle)

Mix butter and lemon juice. In another bowl, mix flour, salt
and pepper. Dip fish in butter mixture, then coat with flour
mix. Use ungreased baking dish. Pour remaining butter over
fish and sprinkle with paprika. Cook uncovered in 350 degree
oven for 25 to 30 minutes.

Ervena Ames, Thomaston, Maine

Creamed Codfish

2 cups milk
2 tablespoons butter
2 tablespoons flour
grated cheese (sprinkle)
Fresh bread crumbs (about ¼ cup)
3/4 cup codfish, shredded

Mix milk,flour and butter together in saucepan, blend until smooth.
Mix 1 cup cream sauce with codfish; pour into a well-greased baking
dish. Sprinkle with bread crumbs and grated cheese. Dot with butter
and bake in moderate oven (375 degrees) for 15 to 20 minutes, until
the crust is a delicate brown. Good served with baked potatoes.

Fish Casserole

½ pound scallops, chopped
1 can shrimp soup
3/4 pound haddock, small pieces
½ can evaporated milk
dash salt and pepper

Combine all ingredients, except bread crumbs. Place in a baking dish. Top with buttered crumbs, and bake in 350 degree oven for 40 minutes. Serves 6.

E. Virginia Glass, Belfast, Maine

Broccoli Casserole-Good with Fish

2 packages frozen chopped broccoli
1 stack ritz crackers
8 ounces Velveeta Cheese
¼ pound butter or margarine

Cook and drain broccoli. Put half in casserole. Dot with half the butter. Add remaining broccoli and cover with slices of cheese. Sprinkle crushed ritz crackers on top. Melt remaining butter and pour over top. Bake in 350 degree oven for 30 min.

Ervena Ames, Thomaston, Maine

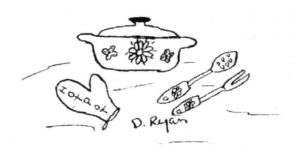

Halibut Steaks with Sauce

3 to 4 pounds halibut steaks

1 teaspoon wine

½ stick butter (softened)

3 tablespoons mayonaise

½ cup grated parmesian cheese

2 dashes tabasco sauce

2 tablespoons onion, grated

2 tablespoons pepper, green grated

½ teaspoon salt

1 tablespoon horseradish

Mix all ingredients. Broil fish; if it is a thick steak cook fish on both sides until almost done. Then put sauce on each side and cook for 3 minutes. Make sure both sides are cooked with sauce on it.

Halibut Fillet

Arrange small broiled fillets of halibut, or flounder on a hot platter, pour a good cream or drawn butter sauce on it, and garnish with watercress or parsley.

Halibut Supreme

Cream sauce or white thin sauce

1 tablespoon lemon juice

1 teaspoon onion, minced

1 small carrot

1 bay leaf

2 pounds halibut

buttered cracker crumbs

Boil fish in salted water, and vegetables, also, seasonings. Cook until fish flakes easily. Drain, flake,and lay in a shallow greased glass baking dish; generously grease with butter. Pour over it a well seasoned rich cream or white sauce. Top with buttered cracker crumbs and bake in a 450 degree oven until golden brown top.

Lobster or Crabmeat Skillet Meal

Great Skillet Meal-breakfast-lunch or dinner

Take one well seasoned iron skillet, put oleo, butter or bacon fat in pan. Take leftover lobster or fresh crabmeat , break up and let simmer awhile. Break 6 eggs in a bowl and stir, Do not over cook. Add salt and pepper or whatever desired. Serve with hot biscuits, and/or toast. Great Sunday a.m. Brunch.

Frank Gilley, Maine Guide, Brewer, Maine

Lobster Casserole

1½ cups lobster meat
1 cup milk
1 cup soft bread crumbs
1 egg, well beaten
½ teaspoon dry mustard
2 tablespoons butter
1 tablespoon lemon juice
crushed corn flakes

Combine all ingredients in baking dish and top with crushed corn flakes. In 350 degree oven for 1 hour.

Ervena Ames, Thomaston, Maine

Broiled Mackerel

Split whole fish down the back, dry thourghly, sprinkle with salt, pepper, and parsley, then the lemon juice very slowly. Dip in salad oil or brush with melted butter. Place fish, flesh-side down toward the flame, on a broiler. After 5 minutes turn and broil on skin-side until crisp and brown. Cover with melted butter, and serve at once.

Baked Oysters

1 dozen oysters
salt and pepper to taste

Over each oyster spread ½ teaspoon horseradish. Mix 3/4 cup of cracker or bread crumbs with 1 tablespoon melted butter, and spread over oysters. Broil or bake 10 minutes.

Wrapped Oysters

Use large oysters and wrap each one in a thin strip of bacon. Place in a pan with bacon-ends under the oyster. Bake in a oven (quick) until the bacon is crisp. Serve immediately.

Oysters and Green pepper

2 dozen oysters
1 teaspoon green pepper, minced
salt and pepper, sprinkle
lemon juice, few drops
bacon,

Wash and open oysters. Over each oyster pour a few drops of lemon juice, finely mince green pepper, and a square of bacon. Sprinkle with salt and pepper. Bake in 450 degree oven for 10 or 12 minutes, or under the broiler for 5 minutes.

E. Virginia Glass, Belfast, Maine

Salmon Cutlets

1 pound salmon
1 tablespoon flour
salt and pepper to taste

Cook, drain and flake salmon and add the flour and seasonings.
Shape in any desired way and fry on a hot griddle or in a greased
frying pan. Serve with slices of lemon or fresh tomatoes.

Salmon Loaf

1 pound red or pink salmon
1/3 cup salmon liquid
1 cup bread crumbs
1 teaspoon dry mustard
½ cup chopped onion
2/3 cup milk
1 egg, beaten
½ teaspoon salt

Boil Salmon until done, drain liquid and save. Flake; and add onion
and mix. Add remaining ingredients and mix thouroughly. Put salmon
mixture into a 9x5 inch greased loaf pan or 2 qt. casserole dish.
Bake in 350 degree oven for 40 to 50 minutes or until firm in center.
If to be sliced, let stand 5 minutes for easier slicing.

E. Virginia Glass, Belfast, Maine

Broiled Scallops

Scallops
Butter, 2 tablespoons
Bread or cracker crumbs, (sprinkle)
Garlic salt, paprika, (sprinkle)
sherry

When using large-sized scallops, slice horizontally through center.
Place scallops in an oven pan containing butter and sherry. Sprinkle
with topping made of crumbs, garlic salt, and paprika. Dot with butter
and broil until done (about 5-7 minutes.) Serve with lemon wedges.

Fried Scallops

2 pounds scallops
¼ cup butter, melted
1 clove garlic, minced
½ cup chopped parsley
salt and pepper, (sprinkle)

Brown garlic in butter, Add scallops; cook 5 to 7 minutes. Stir often.
Sprinkle with salt and pepper. Add parsley and cook 1 minute longer,
or until transparent. Serve hot.

Roxanne B. Carter, Swanville, Maine

Baked Trout

Salt & pepper

Onion, sliced

Fresh garlic clove, minced

Trout cleaned, rinsed

I can of diced tomatoes

- Rub salt and pepper over cleaned and rinsed trout
- Stuff trout with sliced onion and garlic
- Lay down a bed of sliced onion in a I3x9 baking dish, on top of the onion add 3-4
- pieces of uncooked bacon, and 2-3 bay leaves, place the trout on top of the
- onion, bacon, and bay leaves
- Add more sliced onion over top of trout
- Pour 1 can of diced tomatoes over top of the trout
- Bake in a 375 degree preheated oven until trout is tender (approximately 15 minutes)

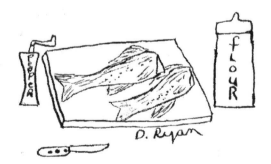

D. Ryan

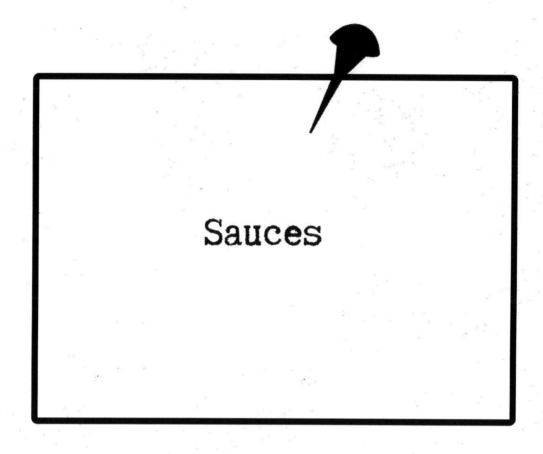

Sauces

Cheese Sauce

3 tablespoons butter	½ teaspoon salt
¼ cup flour	Cayenne pepper
1½ cups hot milk	6 ounces processed cheese

Melt the butter in a sauce pan; add the flour and rub to a paste, gradually adding the hot milk; stir and cook until thick; add the salt, a few grains of cayenne pepper; remove from the stove and add the processed cheese, which melts without becoming stringy and tough; stir until the mixture is smooth. Serve over fish.

Cocktail Sauce

8 tablespoons ketchup	3 tablespoons lemon juice
2 tablespoons horseradish	¼ teaspoon celery salt

Tobasco sauce to taste

Mix in bowl slightly, then place in a wide mouthed bottle and shake until thoroughly mixed. Good served in cocktail glasses over cooked lobster meat. May add a extra tablespoon of lemon juice for tartness.

Egg Sauce

2 cups hot milk	4 tablespoons melted butter
4 tablespoons unbleached flour	½ teaspoon salt
¼ teaspoon pepper	2 hard-boiled eggs

Blend melted butter and flour well. Add hot milk and cook until thick on medium heat. Slice hard-boiled eggs and add to sauce. Serve with boiled fish.

Lobster Sauce

1 cup milk	3 tablespoons flour
½ cup cream	1 teaspoon salt
3 tablespoons melted butter	¼ teaspoon pepper

1 to 1½ cups fresh cooked lobster

Blend melted butter, flour and seasonings and stir steadily until thoroughly . Pour milk and cream in gradually, and simmer for 2 minutes. Add chunks of fresh cooked lobster. Heat; not boiling.

Tartar Sauce

1 cup mayonnaise	1 tablespoon minced onion
1 tablespoon minced sweet pickles	
1 tablespoon minced parsley	

Mix thoroughly; and serve cold. For fried fish, pan fried oysters,etc.

Drawn Butter

1½ cups hot water
1/3 cup butter
3 tablespoons flour
¼ teaspoon pepper
¼ teaspoon salt

Melt half the butter, add flour, salt and pepper; mix, and gradually add hot water. Boil 5 to 10 minutes; add remaining butter. Use to dip lobster in, good.

Lemon Sauce

¼ cup butter, melted
¼ teaspoon pepper
1 to 1¼ teaspoons lemon juice

Blend ingredients in saucepan, serve hot over lobster meat.

Thin White Sauce

3 cups milk
3½ tablespoons butter
1½ teaspoons salt
3 tablespoons flour
dash pepper

Melt butter over low heat. Stir in flour, salt and pepper; adding milk gradually, keep stirring while cooking over low heat, until sauce thickens. Serve warm over broiled fish.

Cucumber Sauce
½ cup whipping cream
¼ teaspoon salt
a few grains pepper
2 tablespoons vinegar
1 large cucumber

Whip cream until stiff; adding salt, cayenne, vinegar, and cucumber, which has been pared, cut fine, and drained. Serve with salmon.

E. Virginia Glass, Belfast, Maine

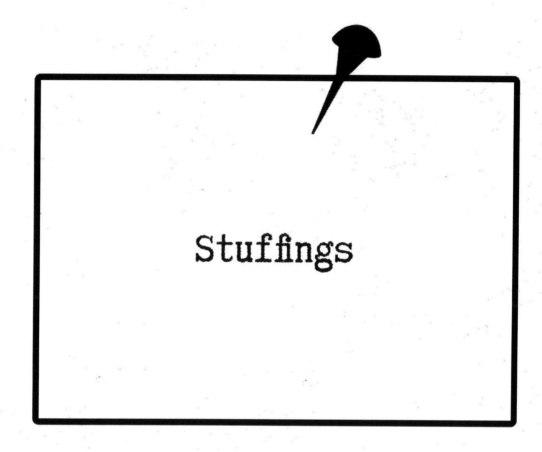

Stuffings

Baked Bass or Pike Stuffing

4 cups bread, cubed

1 teaspoon crushed sage leaves

½ teaspoon salt

¼ teaspoon pepper

2 stalks celery cooked, chopped fine

4 tablespoons liquid from celery

6 tablespoons hot melted butter

3 tablespoons onion, minced

Cleanse fish, and fill with stuffing. Sew up and cover with salt
pork slices then, dredge with flour. Add 1 cup boiling water in
shallow pan and lay fish in this and bake 1 hour; baste frequently.
Remove the fish when done, add browned flour and butter to the
gravy, cook a few minutes, then pour around fish on platter; sprinkle
with parsley.

Bread Stuffing

Large loaf bread, cubed

1 teaspoon salt, thyme, sage,

Dash pepper

1/3 cup melted butter

½ cup chopped celery

¼ cup onion, chopped

Cook celery and onion in butter until they are tender. Combine all
ingredients; mix thoroughly. If stuffing seems dry, add 1 tablespoon
fish stock to moisten. Good with yellow perch fillets, or other fish
fillets.

Crab Filling

1 cup crab meat	2 eggs
2 cans chicken soup	1 cup cheese(cut up fine)
1 pint milk	1/8 lb. butter

Melt cheese, add soup and milk with eggs beaten in it. Thicken
with flour; add crabmeat and serve. Good on toasted English Muffins.

Ervena Ames, Thomaston, Maine

Seafood Stuffing with Crab and Scallops

1 pound crabmeat
10 ounces scallops
1 small box ritz crackers
3 eggs
1½ sticks butter
evaporated milk
salt and pepper to taste

Combine drained crabmeat,scallops finely chopped or shredded, crushed ritz crackers, eggs, melted butter and enough evaporated milk to make very moist. Salt and pepper to taste and stuff fish, or eat by itself, this will make your tastebuds cry for more!

Roxanne B. Carter, Swanville, Maine

Oyster Stuffing

2 cups bread cubes
1 teaspoon salt
¼ teaspoon pepper
1 tablespoon onion, minced
1 stalk celery, diced
4 tablespoons melted butter
1 pint oysters

Use stale bread. Cut in ½-inch squares, rather than make into crumbs. Add melted butter, and stock in which onion and celery have been cooked until tender. Mix well with a fork. Look over oysters to remove bits of shell.

Crabmeat Stuffing

5 ounces crabmeat(fresh is better)   1 cup chopped chives
3 tablespoons fresh or dried parsley,minced
2 tablespoons butter   ¼ cup soaked bread crumbs
2 tablespoons Worcestershire sauce   dash salt and pepper
½ cup dry wine

Saute' in butter chives until soft and lightly brown. Squeeze out excess water from bread and crumble. Add remaining ingredients, stir gently and cook on low heat, and cool. Place in glass dish, cover with plastic wrap and refrigerate until needed.

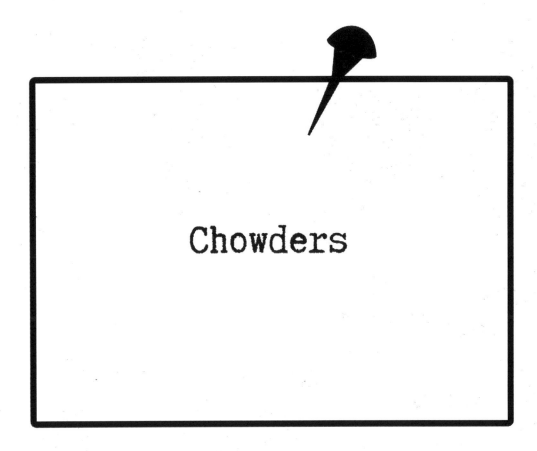

Chowders

58

Clam Chowder

2 cups clams, chopped
1 can evaporated milk
5 potatoes, cubed
2 tablespoons butter

1 pint milk
1 cup clam juice
1 small onion, diced

Brown onion in butter, add clams, clam juice and potatoes, simmer until cooked. Add milk; heat and serve.

E. Virginia Glass, Belfast, Maine

Codfish Chowder

2 cups milk
½ cup water
4 large potatoes
pepper and salt to taste
3 pounds fresh codfish

2 cups evaporated milk
2 tablespoons butter
2 onions, diced
1 small piece salt pork

Skin, and remove head, tail and backbone. Cut into small pieces, place in covered saucepan with salt to taste and cold water; cook 20 minutes. Drain; save juice. Cut salt pork into small pieces. Dice onions, and fry salt pork and onions together for 5 minutes. Strain off fat. Dice potatoes, and cook for 5 minutes, add other ingredients and cook for 10 minutes. Serve with hot biscuits.

E. Virginia Glass, Belfast, Maine

Crabmeat Stew

4 cups milk
1 cup water
½ teaspoon salt
2 to 2 ½ cups fresh crabmeat

1 can evaporated milk
3 tablespoons butter
¼ teaspoon pepper

Melt butter and saute' crabmeat, remembering it is best to melt butter slowly. Add water to mixture and boil 1 minute. Pour in milk, stir until hot, but do not boil. Add salt and pepper and evaporated milk. Rehaeat, but care not to boil.

Sheila B. Howie, Belfast, Maine

Haddock Chowder

½ to 1 can evaporated milk
4 med. potatoes, diced
3 slices salt pork

1 med. onion, quartered
salt and pepper to taste
1 pound haddock fillet, cubed

Cook potatoes and onions in kettle with hot water enough to cover.
Place fish fillet, cubed on top . When done remove any remaining
bones and the skin. Add fat, and evaporated milk and seasoning.
It's best to cook salt pork separately for fat. Reheat, do not
boil, and serve. Good with buttered crackers.

Seafood Chowder

1 pint clams, chopped
½ pound scallops, cut up
1 cup crabmeat
1 small onion, diced
3 cups potatoes, diced
2 slices salt pork

2 cups lobster, cooked
2½ cup fresh shrimp, cooked
2 quarts milk, scalded
½ cup butter
2 cups water

Fry salt pork and save fat to cook diced onion. Add water and
potatoes, cover and cook about 15 minutes. Place scallops on'
potatoes, simmer until scallops are done. If clams are uncooked,
place them in kettle at same time. Add remaining seafood, and
scalded milk, and butter.Salt and pepper for seasoning.

Roxanne B. Carter, Swanville, Maine

Lobster Chowder

1½ to 2 pounds lobster,cooked
1 large onion,diced
2 teaspoons salt
2 cups milk

¼ cup butter
4 medium potatoes, cubed
¼ teaspoon pepper
2 cups evaporated milk

Cut cooked lobster meat in large pieces. Saute lobster in butter
until meat has rosy color. Fry salt pork, add onion and cook until
slightly brown. In kettle, combine salt pork fat, onion, potatoes
and add water to barely cover. Cook until potatoes are tender. Add
lobster, milk and evaporated milk, salt and pepper. For more rich-
ness in stew, add half and half or cream in place of evaporated milk.

E. Virginia Glass, Belfast, Maine

Salmon Chowder

1 pound salmon, fresh-cleaned and deboned

1-quart milk

1 small onion, diced

2 tbsp. butter

2 tbsp. all-purpose flour

2 potatoes, cubed

Salt & pepper, to taste

1. In a medium-size double boiler cook fresh salmon with milk, onion, and potatoes for about 25 minutes or until salmon tests done and vegetables are fork tender.

2. In a bowl blend butter and flour, use this mixture to thicken the chowder. Add salt and pepper to taste.

This is an easy and delicious recipe. Adjusts amounts for the number of servings desired. Serve with your favorite homemade bread, popovers, or biscuit recipe.

Clarence Brown Sr., Belfast, Maine

 **lams**

My Favorite Recipes

Clam Chowder ('Chowdah' in Maine speak)

3 slices salt pork (cubed), or bacon (diced)
1 cup cooked, shelled, clams
1 cup clam juice
Small onion, diced
4 large potatoes, cut-up in small cubes
1 can evaporated milk
1 cup milk
¼ to ½ cup cream
2 tbsp. butter
Salt and pepper to taste

- Fry salt pork or bacon, add onion then some of the clam juice so, that onions won't stick. Cook until soft.

- Add 4 large potatoes (cut-up in small cubes), to the salt pork or bacon and onion mixture. Add extra water if needed but just enough to cover potatoes. Bring to a boil then turn down to a gentle simmer cooking potatoes in clam juice and water until fork tender. Add clams about 15 minutes before done.

- In a medium size pan, add can of evaporated milk plus 1 cup of milk, ¼ to ½ cup cream, and butter, heat the milk to almost boiling, but do not scorch. Take off heat. Add cooked potatoes and clams, gently stir to mix. Serve in bowls with a dot of butter. Salt and pepper to taste.

Tips:

- Chowdah is better if given time to sit awhile, next day after refrigerated overnight has added flavor.
- Adjust clams and milk according to a number of servings you would like to have.
- Bacon can be used in place of salt pork.
- Being a Mainer, I use whatever potatoes I have on hand. Though I have heard that if you use russet potatoes, you don't have to use flour that is an ingredient in some recipes. I omit the flour in my recipe and find this chowder to be scrumptious.
- Use real butter, no substitutes.

— VW

 bster

My Favorite Recipes

Lobster Salad

16 ounces cooked lobster meat, cut into small pieces

1/4 cup mayonnaise

1 celery stalk, diced (optional)

Salt & Pepper to taste

4 top-sliced hot dog buns

Lettuce (optional)

Butter (If grilling is desired)

INSTRUCTIONS

In a large bowl mix together the mayonnaise, celery, salt, and pepper. Add the lobster and hand stir until lobster is coated with mayonnaise. Yessah! Lobster salad is done.

- If you want to eat the lobster salad roll cold, you can line each roll with a lettuce leaf then add lobster mixture and serve.
- Or, you can omit the bread and just have a bed of lettuce for your lobster salad.
- If you want the sandwich grilled, fill each roll with the lobster mixture, butter (each side) of the outside of the roll, and grill on medium heat until golden brown.

Note:

Many lobster salad recipes call for other ingredients such as lemon juice, parsley, chives, or tarragon. My family prefers not adding the extras in our lobster salad and often will leave out the celery. We love the taste of lobster, so the extras in our opinion are not needed. We also prefer the lobster rolls grilled and feel if you don't eat it that way, you are missing out.

—VW

Desserts

My Favorite Recipes
-Whoopie Pies-

Summary: Whoopie Pies are one of my family's favorite desserts, one that they ALWAYS ask me to bake whenever we all get together. Whoopie Pies are easy to make, just time consuming— so set aside a whole afternoon for making this old-fashioned wicked good New England treat!

Ingredients
- 1 1/2 c. shortening or butter
- 3 c. w. granulated sugar
- 6 eggs
- 1 c. dark baking cocoa
- 7 c. +/- unbleached all purpose flour
- 3 tsp. baking powder
- 3 tsp. baking soda
- 2 tbsp. pure vanilla
- 3 c. milk - 3 tbsp.
- 1 1/2 tsp. salt (optional)

Instructions
- In large mixing bowl cream butter, sugar, and eggs
- In separate bowl mix cocoa, flour, baking powder, and baking soda.
- Add flour mixture two cups a time, after each flour addition add 1 cup of milk. The batter will be thick.
- Line a baking sheet with parchment paper and spoon a heaping tablespoon of the batter on the baking sheet, spacing your whoopie pie batter 2 inches apart.
- Bake in preheated 375 F degree oven for ten minutes.
- Take out of the oven and let cool on baking sheet before removing to cooling rack.
- Frost one side of a whoopie and put the cover on.
- Wrap each pie in wax paper, then put in a plastic bag or another airtight container.

Filling

- 1 ½ cups shortening or butter
- 6 c. powdered (confectioner's) sugar
- 6 egg whites
- 6 tsp. pure vanilla extract
- Pinch of salt

This makes for a large batch of Whoopie pies!

Your Favorite Recipes

Your Favorite Recipes

Notes

Notes

INDEX OF RECIPES

Cooking Tips & Tricks

Camper's Specials

Bear

Deer

Rabbit

INDEX OF RECIPES

INDEX OF RECIPES

Stuffings:

Chowders:

Baking Times:

Sec. - Seconds

M - minutes

hr - hour

lb. - pound

Temperatures and Degrees:

Roasts:

Fowl - (slow oven) - 300 Degrees - 2 to 4 hrs (depending on age of fowl).

Venison - (rare - moderate oven) - 350 Degrees - 18 to 20 M per lb.

Venison - (med. - moderate oven) - 350 Degrees - 22 to 25 M per lb.

Venison - (well done - moderate oven) - 350 Degrees - 27 to 30 M per lb.

Simmer - 180 Degrees F
Boil   - 212 Degrees F
Slow oven - 300 - 325 Degrees F
Moderate oven - 350 - 375 Degrees F
Moderately hot oven - 375 - 400 Degrees F
Hot oven - 400 - 450 Degrees F

...watie or tomato ...
... with boiled potatoes, carrots ...
... can also be used for deer meat or ...
... you can use cuts that are a little tougher to ...
steak.

Good Luck with your Cook Book!

Bud Dilldent

My compliments
and congratulations.
I'm proud of you.
Charlie Z.

VIRGINIA WRIGHT is a multi-genre best-selling author and award-winning illustrator of children's books. Wright was a preschool teacher and a licensed childcare worker. In 1981 she sold her first writing to a regional Maine magazine. Wright began writing professionally in 2000, for Lowfat Weekly a then popular nutrition and recipe website that Wright founded. After getting a great response from the kid's corner on her website, in 2007 she started writing and illustrating children's books.

As an illustrator, the cover Wright designed for Steampunk Alice by Dennis Higgins won the AUTHORSdb Gold Award (2014).

Wright won the AUTHORSdb Silver Award (2016) in the cover contest from Timothy the Christmas Mouse Coloring Book for children.

She spent several years as a beekeeper and used that experience to write a nonfiction book, Buzzzzzzzz What Honeybees Do, ranked #1 Amazon Best Seller in three categories (2016).

Steampunk Alice

Contact, Friend or Follow
Facebook: facebook.com/virginiabrownwright
Twitter: twitter.com/virginia_wright
Instagram: instagram.com/wright.virginia
Website: virginiawright.com

More books by this author available online:
http://www.amazon.com/author/virginiawright
http://www.barnesandnoble.com
http://www.booksamillion.com

Made in the USA
Columbia, SC
23 November 2018